Of Bees and Boys:
Lines from a Southern Lawyer
Essays
Allen Mendenhall

Critical Praise for the Prose of Allen Mendenhall

"*Of Bees and Boys: Lines from a Southern Lawyer* is a delicious trip through a marvelous brain. Allen Mendenhall is the most literary of lawyers. He might have been a character out of Twain or Faulkner or his beloved Harper Lee explaining eternal truths to youngsters so they can understand and remember them. But he is real, and he opens his prolific mind in these joyous pages. If you are not from the South and want a slice of breezy southern life seen through the eyes of a master storyteller, read this book. If you are from the South, no doubt you will find a small piece of your personal history in here. I loved these tales so much, I read them twice – and I am from New Jersey."
-Hon. Andrew P. Napolitano, Senior Judicial Analyst, Fox News Channel, Distinguished Visiting Professor of Law, Brooklyn Law School

"This is a book for everyone who likes to think, who wants to contemplate the great questions of life, and most happily, for people who like to read."
-William Bernhardt, *New York Times* bestselling novelist, author of *Challengers of the Dust* and *The Ocean's Edge*

"Allen Mendenhall is a natural storyteller. With the dark humor and wisdom of Mark Twain, he weaves tales of his Southern past: boys wage war on yellow jackets; a grandfather reveals truths about an Alabama author and the characters in her famous novel; a young man faces cancer and his own mortality. This remembered world is the Deep South, a place that holds fast to traditional values and the virtues of family, community, and religion. *Of Bees and Boys* invites the reader to enter this world and, for a while, become part of it."
-Julia Nunnally Duncan, author of *A Place That Was Home* and *A Part of Me*

"From another Southern lawyer, from bees to frogs, yellow jackets and possums, cancer and death, 'What is the meaning of life?' is explored in this collection of essays. Fascinating reading."
-Hon. Thomas L. Waller, Kentucky Circuit Judge, Retired

"Allen Mendenhall possesses a mighty brain and a deep soul. He also wields a powerful pen and knows the power of the word (and the Word). From stoicism to southernism, from bees to Freud, from gossip to incarceration, and from wiretaps to existentialism, Mendenhall leaves few things unexamined. In this gorgeous collection of essays, Mendenhall ably and eloquently gives proof as to why he is one of the most important rising minds in America."
-Bradley J. Birzer, Russell Amos Kirk Chair in History, Hillsdale College

Cover and Interior Design: Greg Gilpin, Graphic Art Center, Inc.
Cover Photo: Greg Gilpin, Graphic Art Center, Inc.
www.graphicartcenter.com

Red Dirt Press
1831 N. Park Ave.
Shawnee, OK 74804
www.reddirtpress.net

ISBN 13: 978-0-692-88894-0

Also by Allen Mendenhall

*The Southern Philosopher: Collected Essays of
John William Corrington* (editor)

*Oliver Wendell Holmes Jr., Pragmatism, and the Jurisprudence of
Agon: Aesthetic Dissent and the Common Law*

Literature and Liberty: Essays in Libertarian Literary Criticism

CONTENTS

CONTENTS

Acknowledgments

I wish to thank the following publications in which earlier versions of these essays first appeared:

"Of Bees and Boys" originally appeared in *Front Porch Republic* and was reprinted in *Red Truck Review*.

"Unmasking" originally appeared in *Kestrel: A Journal of Literature and Art*.

"Are Lawyers Illiterate?" originally appeared in *The Imaginative Conservative*.

"Harper Lee and Words Left Behind" originally appeared in *story-South* and was reprinted in *Red Truck Review*.

"Power Made Perfect in Weakness" originally appeared in *Front Porch Republic*.

"Is Hacking the Future of Scholarship?" originally appeared in *Pacific Standard*.

"Teaching Behind Bars" originally appeared in *Birmingham Arts Journal* and was reprinted as "Beneath the Guard Tower" in *Furman Magazine*.

"To Educate in the Permanent Things" originally appeared in *The American Spectator* and was reprinted in *The Imaginative Conservative*.

Foreword

The cliché, of course, is that lawyers can't write. Criticism of legal writing has become ubiquitous. The word "legalese," a derogatory term for obscure legal verbiage, has become so familiar that it was recently the answer to a question on *Jeopardy*. (And one of the contestants knew it.) I've been teaching legal writing seminars for more than a decade now, so I'm speaking from the front lines when I say that there is some merit to this criticism. The problem, though, derives not from the writing skills lawyers innately possess, but from how lawyers are taught to employ them. Cutting-and-pasting tends to perpetuate archaic writing. Adopting an affected highbrow tone strikes some as more lawyerly – even if it is painfully difficult to read.

None of that is true for Allen Mendenhall, thank goodness. Mendenhall is an artist and writer of the first caliber. His talent shines brightly in even the simplest of sentences. Other lawyer scribes have managed to escape the professional taint by retreating to fiction, but Mendenhall accomplishes even more in the world of nonfiction. The wide-ranging collection of essays in this book, some relating to the law and others on altogether disparate subjects, reveals a probing mind unchecked by subject matter, and an astonishing gift for the written word. Mark Twain is said to have written, "The difference between the almost right word and the right word is the difference between a lightning bug and lightning." Time and again, Mendenhall harnesses the lightning.

Mendenhall opens the book with "Of Bees and Boys," which at first seems a charming and harmless recollection of childhood mischief, but soon becomes something far graver. At the conclusion, this nostalgic reverie has become a meditation on the nature of life and masculinity. Equally powerful is "Unmasking," an essay on death, how we deal with it, and the horror of being diagnosed with cancer at age twenty-four. Despite the dour subject, the essay is filled with wonderful bits of character observation. "Martin loved cigarettes, which he called the backbone of Southern economy and which, he readily admitted, had brought about his three fatalities." Miraculously, this somber subject concludes with possibly the most upbeat passage about death ever written: "[I]t's a sweet but unhappy release, a deliverance, an unmasking. Almost paradoxically, it's freedom within – and despite – limitation."

These are only a few of the treasures in this volume. There is also an analysis of *To Kill a Mockingbird* worthy of publication in a scholarly literature journal, and several incisive pieces on education every teacher should read. Perhaps the most original essay in the book is "On Ugliness." The author is inspired by the sight of a spider's corpse, and from that grim starting point, launches startlingly original thought about what it means to be beautiful, or ugly, and finds both in the most unlikely places.

This is a book for everyone who likes to think, who wants to contemplate the great questions of life, and most happily, for people who like to read.

- William Bernhardt

Of Bees and Boys

My brother Brett and I were polite but rambunctious children who made a game of killing bees and dumping their carcasses into buckets of rainwater. Having heard that bees, like bulls, stirred at the sight of red, we brandished red plastic shovels, sported red t-shirts, and scribbled our faces in red marker. They were small, these shovels, not longer than arm's length. And light, too. So light, in fact, that we wielded them with ease: as John Henry wielded a hammer or Paul Bunyan an axe.

The bees had a nest somewhere within the rotting wood of our swing set. Monkey bars made of metal triangles, much like hand percussion instruments, dangled from the wooden frame above; when struck or rattled with a stick, these replied in sharp, loud tones, infuriating the bees, a feisty frontline of which launched from unseen dugouts.

These deployments, though annoying, were easily outmaneuvered: Brett and I swatted them to the ground with our shovelheads. Mortally wounded, they twitched and convulsed, moving frantically but going nowhere; all except one bee, valiant as he was pathetic, wriggling toward his nearest companion, his maimed posterior dragging in the dirt. Not much for voyeurism, I relieved him of his misery. Then Brett and I whacked the littered lot into tiny bee pancakes.

Meanwhile, the defeated community, convening somewhere in the wood, commissioned its combat medics: fat, steady-flying drones that hovered airborne over the dead and then descended, slow and sinking, like flying saucers. The medics would, when we let them, carry off their dead to an undisclosed location. I couldn't watch this disturbingly human ritual, so instead I annihilated the medics, too. They were easy targets, defenseless. And they kept coming in battalions of ten or eleven. As soon as I'd destroy one battalion, another materialized to attend to the *new* dead. Unlike the frontliners, the medics didn't try to sting. They just came to collect. But I wouldn't let them. Neither would Brett. Eventually, they quit coming. That, or we killed them all.

🐝

Bees are funny creatures. Unlike birds, they have two sets of wings. Most female bees, unlike most female humans I know, grow their leg hairs long and their bellies plump – this in order to carry nectar or pollen. Bee pollination accounts for one-third of the human food supply. Without bees, then, we might not have our Big Macs or Whoppers – nor, for that matter, honey or flowers.

When I lived in Japan, I had a friend who fancied himself an entomologist. When he and I tired of talking politics, books, or women, we spoke of insects: I told him weird insect stories, and he explained away the weirdness. He informed me, for instance, that the bees living in my swing set were probably solitary bees: a gregarious species that stung only in self-defense. This, you might imagine, was sobering news for an insect murderer.

I asked about the medics that carried away the dead. Honey bees, he said, discarded their dead for hygienic reasons – to prevent the spread of infection – and they coated their dead in antibacterial waxes. As for the behavior of my bees, however, he wasn't sure: maybe they, like honey bees, discarded remains where germs wouldn't spread. Or maybe – and he said this facetiously – they conducted funerals.

🐝

It wasn't long before Jared, the boy next door, got in on our bee brutality. Pregnant with mischief – more so than me or Brett – he decided one day to show us something; shepherding us through the woods, lifting a disarming smile as if to say, "Trust me," he paused at last, indicated a hole in the ground, and declared, "This is it!"

A steady stream of yellow jackets purred in and out of the hole. He waved his hand to signify the totality of our surroundings and said, "Ours. *All* ours. None for the bees."

Or something to that effect.

Brett and I nodded in agreement, awaiting instruction. If we were confused by Jared's deranged sense of prerogative, we didn't show it. Brett found a heavy rock, which I helped him to carry. We dropped it at Jared's feet.

Jared summoned forth a mouthful of mucus and hacked it into the hole. Unfazed, the yellow jackets buzzed in acknowledgment but otherwise ignored the assault. "These guys are in for hell," Jared said of the bees, offended at the ineffectuality of his first strike. He anchored his feet and bent over the rock, which he heaved to his chest and, leaning backwards, rested on his belly; then he staggered a few steps, stopped, and – his face registering *another* thought – dropped the rock to the ground.

"Spit on it!" he ordered.

Brett and I, obedient friends that we were, doctored the rock in spit.

Then Jared undertook to finish the job he'd begun: he bent down, lifted the rock, waddled to the hole, straddled the hole, and dropped the rock. The ground thumped. A small swirl of dust spiraled into miniature tornadoes that eventually outgrew themselves and became one with the general order of things.

"That'll do it," Jared said, clapping his hands together to dry the spit. The colony, its passage blocked, was trapped both inside and out. Those un-entombed bees, rather than attack, simply disappeared.

We rejoiced in our victory. Jared pantomimed conquest, pretending to hold an immense and invisible world Atlas-like over his shoulders. Brett danced. I was so busy watching Jared and Brett that I can't remember what I did.

We didn't know that yellow jackets engineered nests, tunneled hidden passages and backup exits; nor did we appreciate what the tiny zealots were capable of.

It started with trifling harassment: a slight, circling buzz – reconnaissance probably. Then I felt the first sting; looking down, I saw a yellow jacket, curled like a question-mark, bearing into my leg. I spanked it dead. It looked angry – something in the way it moved.

I heard Brett scream. Then Jared. Then saw the ubiquitous cloud of yellow jackets rising in the air, moving as one unit, enveloping us with fatalistic purpose. My ears filled with the steady drone of thrumming wings.

Then, as happens in moments like this, moments of panic, moments when one feels he's lost control, feels some *other* faculty taking over, I submitted to a greater power, which stiffened the muscles of my neck and arms, sent contractions through my calves and thighs, like spasms moving me forward, making me to run, the house, my house, once far away, a small square, growing larger and larger until at last it became a complete, reachable form, the door, my safety, announcing its presence, telling me to *hurry, hurry*. Ahead was a fence. I'd have to jump it. I measured my strides for the leap, which, miraculously, I achieved with the slight assistance of my palms upon the fence-top. I found the doorknob, dove into the kitchen, flung off my clothes. The drone wouldn't go away.

But where was Brett? Not here. Where *was* he? Just then came a voice – "*Allen! What in God's name?!*" – and then mom was beside me, horrified, her eyes growing three-times their normal size; and then she was gone again; somehow I was back at the door, looking outside, at the yard, at mom battling the fleet of yellow jackets, at Brett stuck on the fence top, screaming, his face flushed red – *red!* – his arms leaking blood. *Was* that blood? Or a sore? I couldn't tell.

Mom deposited Brett in the kitchen, stripped him naked, called the doctor. Tweezers. I remember tweezers. Yellow jackets were in his ears and mouth. They were everywhere. Outside, they continued ramming their bodies into the window. I looked out. One hovered there. It looked at me. I looked at it. Insect and Man. Sizing each other up.

※

In light of these memories, I can't help but sense that, no, on account of their nature and characteristics, bees are not the affirmative, happy creatures of some Wordsworthian lyric; that they're too much like us for armistice or reconciliation; that, in fact, we will never see the last of them, as they will never see the last of us. They will live on, as will we.

Let the boys at them, and they at the boys. That's how it ought to be. So alike are the two that it's hard to tell who has the advantage of intelligence. I learned, those many years ago, before the profundity of it all struck me, that wounds can teach the tragic lessons of ignored similarities.

If nothing else, I have come to admire bees for their tenacity and courage in the face of insurmountable power. Theirs is a world of flux, disorder, and death. Their body is a weapon, one that, once used, terminates everything.

Boys war with bees. Bees war with boys. Just another kind of outdoor game, one on a side, except no one can say "Elves." Not in this game.

In this game, there is only one ending. Even in victory, the bees lose. It may take a man to fully understand. And it might just take bees, or something like them, to make a man.

Unmasking

There is no remembrance of former things; neither shall there be any remembrance of things that are to come with those that shall come after.
– Qoheleth 1:11

Southerners are particular about the way they preserve their loved ones; they encourage embalming, for instance, although at one time they shunned it as unconsented-to tampering with the body. Eventually someone decided, rather wisely, that the deceased, had they a choice, would like a genteel display of their "shell." This meant more than sanitization: it meant dressing the dead like ladies or gentlemen on their way to church. Which is precisely where they were going – just before they were buried in the ground. For the most part, Southerners don't cremate. A preacher once told me that the Bible discourages cremation.

In the South – more than in other regions – funerals are hierarchical affairs: one's nearness to the deceased signifies one's importance to the family. This holds for the church and burial service and is especially true if the departed was popular in life. Being closest to the deceased, pallbearers shoulder the weightiest burden.

Nowhere is decorum more important than at a funeral procession. It's unseemly for one who's not party to the procession to fail to bow his head and arrange a grave face as the procession passes. If you're in a vehicle, you pull over to the curb and, so long as it isn't dangerous to do so, take up the sidewalk as if on foot. Quitting the vehicle is, in general, inadvisable if by the time you encounter the procession the hearse is no longer in sight. Or if, alternatively, the weather doesn't permit. If you're *in* line, the modus operandi is ecclesiastic – ordered from clergy to immediate kin, next-of-kin, distant family, friends, and the rest. Losing your place in line is, accordingly, like losing your intimacy with the family, for whom these rituals are carried out.

❦

I was eight when Great-Granddaddy died. Mom piloted me before his open-casket and whispered, "That's not Great-Granddaddy. That's just a shell. Great-Granddaddy's gone to heaven."

I looked down at the *thing*, the shell, the facsimile that seemed uncannily human, and said to myself – perhaps out loud – "That's *not* Great-Granddaddy. That's something else." But the thing appeared real, strange, so nearly alive that it repulsed me. Its eyes, thank God, were closed, but its mannequin face, vacant and plastic, nauseated me.

Mom prodded me away, hollering at my cousin to take me outside. My first brush with death, while necessary, had not imparted a healthy understanding of mortality.

❦

My grandmother, Nina, tried to familiarize me with the inescapable while I was still a boy. Instead of taking me to playgrounds, she took me to cemeteries for what she called "preparations." These outings usually occurred on warm spring afternoons, when azaleas bloomed bright white and pink, when yellow Jessamine vines crawled up walls and fences, when dogwoods yawned inflorescent, and when tulips, still un-beheaded, stretched with impeccable posture. When, in short, nature was doing *anything* but dying.

Nina shared facts about various grave plots, giving the lowdown on so-and-so's passing – "he died in Korea," "he of AIDS," "she during pregnancy," and so forth. When she finished, we fed the swans.

Which attacked me once. I was standing on the riverbank, feeding the once-ugly ducklings by hand just as Nina had taught me, when, like Leda, I was enveloped by a feathered glory of beating white wings. Traumatized, I no longer stood on shore but sat on the roof of the car. To make me feel less sissy, Nina sat on the hood and pretended that she, too, was afraid. It wasn't their size exactly.

20

Nor the way they tussled with graceful wrath. Maybe it was the mask about their swan eyes. I'm *sure* it was that: the concealment, secret identity, veiled feelings.

Just before I got married, my fiancée, Giuliana, flew in from São Paulo to meet my family. After supper, Nina insisted that I drive her through the cemetery. I hadn't been in years but instantly recognized the rod-iron gates that once seemed so colossal. There was the river. The ducks. The swans. In the distance, a family, their heads bowed, stood under a high green tent.

Giuliana was not disturbed by this detour. Quite the contrary: she felt in some way moved. It was as if Nina had invited her into a private, intimate space: one that contradicted this modern world of medical science in which everyone tries to postpone or avert death. In a cemetery one couldn't help but think of decomposition, permanence, the soul. One couldn't help but track the beat of one's heart, measure the inhales and exhales of one's breathing. One couldn't help, that is, but cherish the fact that one's alive.

My cell phone buzzed. An unknown number flashed across the screen. I answered, "Hello?"

"Mr. Mendenhall?"

"Yes."

"Are you in the car?"

"No."

"This is the cancer center at St. Joseph's Hospital. We need you to come in."

I was twenty-four, and about to hear, "You have cancer."

Nothing – not even a Southern upbringing – can prepare you for those three words.

The odd thing about preachers is that, depending on time and place, their company is either most welcome or most unwelcome. When I got the call, the cancer call, my uncle, a preacher, was beside me, and I was, for that, glad. He made me feel the power of presence and companionship: I was *not* alone.

My uncle – Uncle Steve – preaches in the only Southern Baptist church in Chicago. Unlike most Southern Baptist preachers down South, he eschews the noisy and spectacular, preferring, instead, politesse and restraint. Bookish and professorial, his voice nasal, his nose suitably sloped to hold up his saucer-sized spectacles, he loves theology and will tell you as much at the drop of a hat. What with his general softness, he might, with a bit more age, have been mistaken for Truman Capote, with whom, incidentally, his father – my grandfather – had grown up in Monroeville, Alabama.

A man of custom, a student of Latin and Greek, fluent in Russian and French, a former lawyer and journalist, Uncle Steve is uncommonly qualified to carry on the sanctifying traditions of Western Civilization. He is, in short, a gentleman and a scholar. And he was in Atlanta that day, standing in the Varsity parking lot, his belly stuffed full of chili dogs, his ketchup-smudged face like an advertisement for this, the world's largest drive-in restaurant.

I could feel his gaze moving over me and spared him the discomfort of asking what was the matter.

"I have cancer," I said.

As the words issued from my mouth, my chest felt as though someone were driving a stake into it. *Cancer.* That thing *other* people got. *Old* people. Not young and healthy people. Not *me.*

I tried to act normal, but in doing so betrayed what I really felt – terror.

Uncle Steve put his arm around me. "Come on. Let's get to the hospital."

🙘

Every hour on the hour, the employees of St. Joseph's Hospital pray together. These moments, though heavily orchestrated, bring peace to the ill and dying, the sick and suffering. The nurses and doctors who wander the hallways pause while a disembodied, female voice recites the Lord's Prayer, first in English, then in Spanish. *"Our Father, who art in heaven…"* – the words echo off the cold, linoleum tiles – *"hallowed be thy name."*

This was happening when I walked into the waiting room. A nurse, a heavyset black woman with soft eyes, was behind the counter, her necklace, weighed down by a tiny crucified Jesus, dangling

22

at her pillow-like breasts. She whispered, again and again, *amen, amen*, and then, looking up, took me in with those deep knowing eyes, and spoke without speaking. Sunlight streamed through the cool, trapezoid panes of glass in the ceiling, falling across her face and hair at a low angle.

At last the prayer ended. She unfolded her hands and smiled formally. "Good afternoon, how may I help you?"

Responding with "I have cancer" didn't feel right, so I said, "I'm here to see Dr. Danaker."

That was all she needed to know.

"Bless your heart, child," she said. And, for the first time, I got emotional. She hugged me, calling me child again; then, right then, I wanted to *be* a child, wanted her to scoop me into her arms and cradle me, wanted her thick, strong body wrapped around me; but there, too, was Uncle Steve, dignified and collected. I couldn't break down in front of him.

The nurse ushered me into a white, windowless room with expansive tile walls and sat me on a tissue-papered chair, which swished and crackled whenever I readjusted.

There I was. Conscious. Being, yet trying to fathom *not* being. I imagined myself in a coffin, like that horrid shell, Great-Grand-daddy. Which only made things worse, for I knew that, once *in* the coffin, I would have no notion of being there. The problem was *thinking itself.* I couldn't imagine *being* dead because I couldn't imagine *not* imagining.

❧

On Sunday mornings, before church, dad had always made my siblings and me read from the obituaries. This, he said, would acquaint us with the fragility of life. He also thought the best way to learn was from experience. But he'd known only one person who'd experienced death and lived to tell about it – Martin, a friend of the family, who'd apparently died three times and, on the operating table, been revived. Martin loved cigarettes, which he called the backbone of Southern economy and which, he readily admitted, had brought about his three fatalities.

Except Martin didn't put it in those terms. To him, cigarettes had

23

allowed him to float outside his body for a while, to see what death was like. For better or worse, Martin didn't tease a tunnel of light, greet a golden angel, or feel a fluffy cloud: he simply "left" himself and, in a state of utter weightlessness, peered down on his body as would an outside observer. Maybe that's why dad didn't like us talking to Martin about death: Dad wanted us to hear about St. Peter and heaven and departed relatives.

The trouble with Martin was that one never knew when to believe him. Heck, we barely knew who he was. Ephemerally at least, he'd been my aunt's boyfriend; then, when she dumped him, he'd never gone away: he moved in with my other aunt, a single mother, and helped care for my young cousin. Martin was present every Thanksgiving and Christmas, but neither got nor gave gifts. A transplant from North Carolina, he had daughters somewhere – the Carolinas or Virginia – and had graduated from the University of North Carolina at Chapel Hill, an achievement he was quite proud of. He didn't work. Didn't own a car. And didn't have money. His singular ability to access death could've been, for all we knew, lifted from a sci-fi novel. But I believed him.

Ten. That's how old I was when I saw a dead body I wasn't *supposed* to see. A right turn on I-85, heading north, highway stretching to where sky and land sandwiched together. I was in my school outfit, backpack in my lap. Mom was in her tennis getup, checking the rearview mirror. Traffic was slowing and stopping. To my left was a vast gray sheet held up by blank-faced men. Behind it, a woman. Or what was left of a woman. Arms and legs bent at impossible angles; head sagging, possibly unattached; a bloodied skirt lifted by the breeze. Someone's mom. Or sister. Or wife. Or girlfriend. Or daughter. Here one minute, gone the next. This wasn't dignity. This was mean and messy.

Death, they say, is not only universal but also the great leveler: it befalls kings and paupers, rich and poor, wise and foolish. Solomon, Caesar, Constantine, Charlemagne, Napoleon: all died despite their glory in life. What I never understood, and, frankly, still don't, is why people pretend death doesn't happen. The person who ignores death is delusional at best, narcissistic at worst. Death is our sole commonality, the thing in this world we all await, about which we may commiserate. It's what makes us human. One can't fully love a person without knowing that person is temporary.

Francis Bacon once said that the "contemplation of death, as the wages of sin, and passage to another world, is holy and religious; but the fear of it, as a tribute due unto nature, is weak." Weak it may be to the healthy and fit, but to the ill and ailing it seems only natural. The person who claims he doesn't fear death is either a liar or a maniac – or else a coward, too faint-of-heart to face the facts. Bacon himself had the good fortune of dying in two to three days, having contracted pneumonia while conducting an experiment in the snow. Willfully blind to his fate, lying on his deathbed, he penned a letter to his friend, Thomas Howard, expressing relief that he hadn't suffered the fortune of Caius Plinius, "who lost his life by trying an experiment about the burning of Mount Vesuvius."

After surgery, I, like Bacon, was bedridden. Soon a phone call would tell me one of two things: that I was okay, my cancer hadn't metastasized, or I wasn't okay, I needed chemotherapy and my chances of living another two years were below fifteen percent. A glued-together wound, resembling fat, blue, puckered-up lips, took up the length of my chest. Visitors asked to see it and then regretted their request when I rolled up my shirt, revealing a moon-shaped, smurfy smile. When the visitors left, and I was alone again, alone and quiet, I imagined what the malignancy would look like as it spread through my body, which I imagined was a mini mine field: tunneled with small explosive cancer clusters about to be detonated. How could this shell – which once ran a mile in under four-and-a-half minutes – expire?

※

I'm not in my brain but somewhere lower: near the chest, maybe, or the gut. I couldn't, for instance, stop a dream even if I wanted to. Which is odd, because it's *my* brain that's dreaming – not someone else's. The brain works independently of me, or, to be precise, of what I *perceive* to be me: it's like an unmanned motor boat zipping

25

on the water. Occasionally one of my siblings, or an old friend, will recall some long-ago event, which I'd otherwise forgotten, and then, suddenly, I'll remember. The brain has stored this memory somewhere – somewhere not readily accessible – but I, *wherever* I am in this shell, never felt compelled to find it. The thought just exists up there, waiting.

It's the soul, I suppose, that's me. When I lie awake at night and contemplate this interim body, which I inhabit the way a renter lives in an apartment, I locate my self – that subjective knowing ego – whole and center, as though the brain, convenient as it is, has a mind of its own. To be sure, I can borrow this organ when I study or otherwise require deep reflection; but when I tire of thinking, when I want a break, when I lean back from my desk, I'm very aware that *I*, my *self*, am moving from the head to my chest, where I *belong*. And when I experience joy, compassion, anguish, despair – when, that is, I *feel* – it's never with my head but with something deep within my bosom. How does one explain this? Perhaps we're all antecedent to the body: little floating things confined to this definite, corporate form we didn't choose, waiting, like thoughts, to be accessed – or released.

❦

Opossums, more commonly known, in the South, as "possums," are, I'm told, a delicacy. Nina's got a cookbook that says so, though she claims she's never cooked or eaten one.

At seven, I persuaded my brother to take a life. A possum's life. It was a horrible affair. One that, even today, is difficult to own up to. Brett, being the gullible little brother he was – I convinced him once that the shadow-puppet giant who lived on the ceiling would kill him in his sleep – stomped on a squeaking pile of pine-straw while I looked on, presumably to punish him if he disobeyed. Of course, the squeaking didn't belong to the pine-straw but to a tiny nest of baby possums underneath.

For some reason, I was initially proud of what I'd done, and, hours later, said as much to my mom. Horrified, she made me show her the nest, since I'd "cried-wolf" before. Sure enough, there, in the pine-straw, lay a bloody baby possum, whimpering and dying.

My first defense was I hadn't *done* anything. Brett had. I'd simply stood by and watched. Mom was smarter than that. I don't remember what she said – only that, once she said it, I began to cry. And couldn't stop.

It was this event, this murder of an innocent, that brought about my general appreciation for original sin, or at least for the idea of innate human depravity. Humans, you might say, are *born* rotten – so much so that most of us, in our youth, could stomp infant possums to death without understanding the wrongness of our action. No doubt I regretted this behavior – this *actus rea* – but not because I felt guilty: it was, in effect, because I feared punishment – some combination of mom's wrath and her spank-happiness. A parent's role is, among other things, to tame a child's destructive impulses. That's what mom did – without succumbing to her own elemental aggressions.

She called the Chattahoochee Nature Center, a local environmental organization, and a worker there explained how to save the baby possum. This, then, became my task, my agonizing punishment: to keep the possum alive. Being intimate with death is one thing; being intimate with suffering quite another. When I scooped the trembling creature up to my palm, it emitted a sad, pitiable squeak. "Everything's okay," I whispered, "I'm not here to hurt you" – a funny assurance coming from the kid who'd just ordered its murder.

Truth be told, I wished I'd just destroyed the thing. Better dead than in this wretched condition. Still, the way it looked at me – its beady, searching eyes perusing my face – reminded me of how Ansley, my little sister, then only a year old, looked up at mom when she wanted to be fed.

I placed the creature in a shoe box, which I tucked beneath a shelf in my parents' closet, the darkest place in the house. More than anything, the possum needed darkness and silence. I dug a hole in the backyard, tied two twigs together in the shape of a cross, and arranged a constellation of stones around what would've been a grave. But the thing didn't die. It healed so well that, the next morning, it was squirming and scurrying and dad needed a net to contain it. Even after the possum was free in the backyard, I left the grave untouched, a reminder that all things, even possums, eventually come to an end.

❧

My Southern upbringing was all about learning how to die. Like the Greek Stoics, Southerners believe in cultivating virtue, improving life, and accepting mortality. Liberated from urban distractions, tied to land and home, they regard humans as custodians of the past; they keep gardens, preserve antiques, record lineage, mark battlefields, and salvage the efforts of planters, carpenters, raconteurs, and architects; they ensure, in short, the availability of history. This can lead to nostalgia for times they never knew, bad times, ugly times, which is to say this can cause Southerners to overlook – or, worse yet, revise – the inconveniences of history: slavery, for instance, or segregation. Yet the Southern tradition, burdened as it is by conflict, retains virtues worth sustaining: community, family, religion, husbandry, stewardship. These ideals and customs, however vulnerable, need guardians. They will persist, in some form or another, as long as humanity itself; they are permanent ideals – tested by generations – which people fall back on during disorienting times. In a region haunted by racial brutality, these principles are, and have been, a unifying reference point, a contact zone where cultures – black, white, and Hispanic – share something spiritual despite all differences.

Living history, not just studying it, but consciously *living* it, is neither wicked nor wrong; the chronic, urgent awareness that everything you know and love will come undone is not, I think, misguided, but utterly essential. There's something beautiful about facing the insurmountable. When the world's fleeting, death becomes a liberating, if terrifying, reality. It throbs and pulsates and beats beneath the skin, inside of which we're all raw skeleton.

For all this, however, I wasn't ready. Didn't want to die. Couldn't even conceive of it. The twenty-something years my family had been teaching me about death amounted to, not nothing, but not much, either. Death, I suppose, is a hard thing to accept, and an even harder thing to fight, since fighting seems so pointless: deep

28

down, you know you can't win. You might prevail once. Maybe even twice. But ultimately it'll beat you. It almost did me.

※

Friends ask how it feels to "beat" cancer. I never can answer – not satisfactorily – because the experience was more like submission than triumph: it was a manifold process of coming to terms with the body, a thing doomed to decay. When the doctor – Dr. Danaker – called to say the lymph nodes were benign, that the cancer hadn't spread, I shocked him with a tired reply: "Good."

"This is *great* news," he assured me, as if I needed reminding, as if I hadn't appreciated – indeed, hadn't *understood* – how lucky I was.

"I know," I said.

At this, the good doctor seemed annoyed. "Ungrateful kid," his tone implied. But I wasn't ungrateful. Nor ecstatic. I was, simply put, unbound – by life, by people, by things. *His* take was that I had been given another chance, a fresh start, that I could put this tribulation behind me and move on. *My* take was that, having embraced impermanence, I was done protecting myself from suffering, done seeking security through delusion, done dislocating from fate, destiny, providence, what have you.

Done: this, it is true, is weary resignation. Yet it's more than that: it's a sweet but unhappy release, a deliverance, an unmasking. Almost paradoxically, it's freedom within – and despite – limitation.

What's more exhilarating than that one should die? What's more mysterious, more horribly electrifying? As one writer, Paul Theroux, has stated, "Death is an endless night so awful to contemplate that it can make us love life and value it with such passion that it may be the ultimate cause of all joy and all art." That is how you cope with this chilling, daunting, stupefying phenomenon: you do it every day until it's serviceable and aesthetic, until at last you won't know, can't know, when it happens, until it's pleasurable, a masterpiece, sublime in its regularity. You keep it close, so close it becomes part of you, so close it's at your disposal, so close that without it, you're nothing, nothing if not boringly, thoughtlessly, mechanically alive, which is just another way of being dead. You train and train and then it comes.

30

Are Lawyers Illiterate?

Webster's defines "intelligent" as "endowed with intelligence or intellect; possessed of, or exhibiting, a high or fitting degree of intelligence or understanding." This modern understanding of "intelligence" as an innate disposition or propensity differs from earlier understandings of the word as meaning "versed" or "skilled." Milton, for instance, in *Paradise Lost*, calls the eagle and the stork "intelligent of seasons," by which he meant that these birds, because of their experience, were cognizant of the seasons.

The older meaning of "intelligent" has less to do with native endowment than it does with gradual understanding. The older meaning, in other words, is that intelligence is acquired by effort and exposure rather than fixed by biological inheritance or natural capacity: one may become intelligent and is not just born that way; intelligence is a cultivated faculty, not an intrinsic feature.

Because of the altered signification of "intelligent," we use today different words to describe the older meaning: erudite, knowledgeable, informed, traveled, educated. These words seem to us more palatable than their once-favored predecessors: civilized, polished, cultured, genteel, refined. I myself prefer words like "lettered" or "versed" that imply a knowledge of important books and the humanities generally.

The most apt term in this regard is also the most butchered in the current lexicon: "literate." Contrary to what appears to be the prevailing assumption, "literate" does not simply refer to an ability to read. According to *Webster's*, "literate" means "instructed in letters,

31

educated; pertaining to, or learned in, literature."

Not just to read, but to read *well* and *widely* – that is how you become "literate." Accepting this traditional meaning, I question how many lawyers are or can become literate.

In the 1980s, Ithiel de Sola Pool, a professor of communications and media, determined that the average American adult reads approximately 240 words per minute. At that rate, it would take a person around 2,268.36 minutes (or 37 hours, 48 minutes, and 21.6 seconds) to read *War and Peace*, which comes in at 544,406 words. If that sounds encouraging – ever wanted to read *War and Peace* in a day-and-a-half? – consider these offsetting variables: reading at one sitting slows over time; attention span and memory recall are limited; the mind can be exercised only so much before it requires rest; people cannot constantly read for 2,268.36 minutes without going to the restroom or eating or daydreaming, among other things; a healthy lifestyle entails seven to nine hours of sleep per day; large portions of the day are spent carrying out quotidian duties like showering, cooking, brushing teeth, commuting to and from work, getting dressed and undressed, answering phone calls, reading emails, cleaning, filling out paperwork, paying bills, and so on.

Pool, moreover, was not using a text like *War and Peace* to gather his data, and his subjects were not writing in the margins of their books, taking notes on their laptops, or pausing to engage others in critical conversations about some complex narrative.

The National Association for Legal Career Professionals has estimated that lawyers at large firms bill on average 1,859 hours per year and work 2,208 hours per year. These numbers are troubling in view of the fact that large law firms also require their attorneys to attend functions with clients and potential clients, time that is neither billable nor considered "working hours."

If there are around 8,760 hours in a year, and if a healthy person spends about 2,920 of those sleeping, there remain only around 5,840 hours per year for everything else. If "everything else" consisted of nothing – nothing at all – except reading *War and Peace*, then a lawyer at a large law firm could read that book about 154 times a year. But of course this is not possible, because no person can function as a machine functions. Once the offsetting variables are accounted for – and I have listed only a few that immediately spring to mind, and these for people with no families – it becomes apparent that it is nearly impossible for a lawyer to read more than about four lengthy or difficult books each month, and only the most diligent and disciplined can accomplish that.

Numbers can lead us astray, so let us consider some anecdotal evidence – my own testimony – which suggests that most lawyers are illiterate, or perhaps that lawyers have to try really hard to become literate or avoid losing their literacy.

I am a lawyer, one who considers himself literate but increasingly in danger of becoming illiterate the longer I remain in my chosen profession. My hope is that literacy stays with you, that if you "frontload," as it were, you can build a wide enough base to allow for slack in later years.

In 2013, I made an effort to overcome the time restrictions of my job to read through several canonical texts of Western Civilization. For the most part I undertook a book a week, although, because of scheduling constraints, I read what I took to be the most important or most famous sections of the lengthier books and volumes such as Aquinas's *Summa Theologica*, a work that would require years of study to fully appreciate. I found myself, on many Thursday evenings, reading so rapidly to finish the text at hand that I could not enjoy myself or absorb the nuances and complexities established by the author.

Reading only one book a week when you are intelligent enough to read more is shameful and disgraceful, the sacrifice of a gift. During graduate school, I could read five or six books a week and can recall more than one week when I read a book a day. But each day I spend working as a lawyer, I am less able to digest the books I consume and to consume the books necessary for mental nourishment.

Economists use the term "opportunity cost" to refer to a choice to forego options or pursue the benefits of one course of action rather than another. The cost of becoming a lawyer is giving up literacy or making its attainment more difficult; the gain, in theory, is a higher salary and financial stability. Whether the gain neutralizes the loss depends on one's preferences. I myself would not trade for a million dollars the opportunity to read Tolstoy or Shakespeare or Aristotle or Santayana.

To achieve the admiration enjoyed by lawyers, other professionals must do their jobs several times better. Happily, this is not a high bar. That's why people prefer the company of doctors. It's not that lawyers are incompetent or unskilled; it's that they don't put their faculties to good use. All people think, but it is only by degree and the object of their thought that the literate are distinguished from the illiterate. To put their minds to humane use would improve lawyers' reputations considerably and call into question that axiom popularized by one of Dickens's characters: "If there were no bad people, there would be no good lawyers."

The way I see it, you can spend all your life billing clients and pushing paper under great stress, by investing your talents and resources in prospects that yield no intellectual returns, or you can spend your life establishing high standards of reason, understanding, and creativity by studying the most important and influential works that humans have produced through the ages. You can spend all your time transacting business, prosecuting and defending lawsuits, and preparing briefs and memoranda, or you can cultivate discernment and understanding. The options are not mutually exclusive: I have overstated to draw a sharp contrast, but the point remains.

Do not misunderstand me: working hard and earning profits are not only good and healthy but personally fulfilling. Yet they must be supplemented with humane contemplation and the private study of important ideas. Industry and innovation are requisite to a high quality of life, a robust economy, and human flourishing – and they make possible the time and leisure that enable some people to create great art and literature. Not everyone can be literate, and that is a good thing.

It's just that many lawyers never learn to live well and wisely, to place their seemingly urgent matters into perspective, or to appreciate, as Aristotle did, the virtues of moderation. This failure is directly related to lawyers' neglect of history and philosophy and to their suppression of the moral imagination that works of good literature can awaken. This failure, as well, puts lawyers at a distinct disadvantage when it comes to spiritual, moral, and intellectual pursuits. As Mark Twain quipped, "The man who does not read good books has no advantage over the man who cannot read them."

Lawyers are illiterate, most of them anyway. Trust them to handle your real estate closings or manage your negligence claims, to finalize your divorce or dash off angry letters to your competitors, but do not trust them to instruct you on plain living and high thinking. There are exceptions – Gerald Russello and Daniel Kornstein are two – but generally lawyers are not to be consulted on matters of importance to the soul. For those, we have good books, and with luck, the people who write and read them.

Harper Lee and Words Left Behind

Nelle Harper Lee spent her final years embroiled in lawsuits as I awaited the publication of a book she is rumored to have written about an Alabama salesman who got wealthy by murdering multiple wives and collecting the life insurance proceeds. My sources – all reliable people – insisted the book was complete, but I don't know whether it is or will be published. When *Go Set a Watchman* was released in 2015, I thought it was the book I'd been anticipating, but it wasn't. Perhaps Lee and her heirs have more secrets to reveal.

One of my earliest memories is of a bookcase at my grandparents' beach house in Destin, Florida, that held the films my family considered to be classics: *Dr. Zhivago, Patton, Gone With the Wind*, and, among others, *The Sound of Music*. I remember one film above all because it was set off from the others, as if on display: *To Kill a Mockingbird*.

Few books have captivated me as has *To Kill a Mockingbird*. I first read it in elementary school. Too young to understand its complexities, I adored Atticus Finch and decided that I wanted to be a lawyer when I grew up. In high school, I named my dog Atticus. Then my sister got a cat. We named it Scout. Neither animal lived up to its namesake: Atticus was needy and pathetic, Scout skittish and brain-dead.

I was born into the book as others were born into money. My grandfather, Papa, was raised in Monroeville, Alabama, by way of Atmore, Alabama, where he was born in 1929. Because the Depression had hit Papa's family especially hard, a charitable doctor in Atmore delivered Papa for free.

Shortly after Papa was born, Great-Granddaddy moved his family to Monroeville and worked for various car businesses, never earning much money. Papa – tall, strong, and handsome – was something of an athlete. He earned a basketball scholarship to Auburn, left Monroeville for college, graduated, and then served in the U.S. Air Force. In 1955, he married his college sweetheart, Barbara Glenn Farish, my grandmother, whom I call "Nina." Nina and Papa moved to Monroeville, where they lived until 1959. Their stay was short. Within a year, they left for Oklahoma and then returned to Alabama to live in Opelika until they made their final move to Atlanta. Papa's Monroeville days were over, save for his visits to relatives.

Great-Granddaddy, however, lived in Monroeville until his death in 1991, the year his beloved Atlanta Braves made it to the World Series just one season after finishing with the worst record in baseball. I often visited Great-Granddaddy in his small, white-wood house with the gravel driveway and grass basketball court that was littered with pecans from the trees above. Papa's aunt, my Great Aunt Jewel, the only person I'd known who was confined to a wheelchair – she had Polio – lived next door and owned one thousand cats. When I asked mom why Aunt Jewel lived near her brother for so long, mom said, "Health, sweetie."

Monroeville was home to two of the 20th century's greatest authors: Lee, the reclusive author of *To Kill a Mockingbird*, a Pulitzer Prize winner, and a recipient of the Presidential Medal of Freedom, who was born in Monroeville in 1926, and Truman Capote, Lee's friend, schoolmate, and neighbor, who lived in Monroeville until the third grade, at which point he moved to New York City. He continued to summer in Monroeville with his aunts, the "wild-haired" women, as Papa called them. Lee was four years older than Papa. "She was," he would say whenever he was probed about the age difference, "in the 12th grade when I was in the eighth grade."

"Back then," he used to say, referring to his childhood in Monroeville, "there was nothing to do, so kids had to use their imaginations." He told me about how Lee and Capote had, despite their young ages and, in the case of Capote, lack of physical prowess, constructed a tree house with the assistance of Lee's brother, Edwin. "They formed a club up there," Papa said, "and to be in the club you had to do certain things." Papa never said what those things were, but he did say that he had been admitted into the tree house.

I was in the third grade when I went to Great-Granddaddy's funeral in Monroeville. I recall a few things clearly from that weekend: Great-Granddaddy's open-casket, Swing-Low-Sweet-Chariot, and the endless pecans, which I gathered from the yard and placed into an old potato sack. Nina bought the pecans from me for one dollar. I thought I was rich, and in some ways, I was.

I also remember Papa telling stories about Lee and Capote that weekend. I delighted in these and shared them with my teachers, who seemed both impressed and skeptical. Papa said that Lee was a tomboy who wouldn't wear dresses and was always in trouble. She would show up at the grass basketball court in his backyard and play with the boys. His descriptions of the girlhood Lee resemble her own portrayal of Scout Finch, the character Aunt Alexandra chastised for tomboyishness. The narrator of *To Kill a Mockingbird* says that Aunt Alexandra was "fanatical on the subject of [Scout's] attire" and insisted that Scout "could not possibly hope to be a lady if [she] wore britches." Whenever Scout declared that she "could do nothing in a dress," especially not play, Aunt Alexandra would inform her that girls weren't "supposed to be doing things that required pants."

Papa's attitude toward Capote was mixed. He took pride in him, but didn't want to glorify him, either. If I asked Papa to describe the boyhood Truman, he would answer, flatly, "Capote was a weird boy." I had to press him for details, perhaps because he did not want to admit that he and his friends had, as one might expect of seven and eight-year-old boys, teased Capote.

Capote was not like the other kids and didn't fit in. He frequented the drug store with a satchel full of papers and pencils, wearing knickers, stockings, and a funny cap and talking with flute-like intonations. He would sit in the drug store for hours, drinking Coca-Cola and producing paper after paper from his satchel, scribbling lines of prose and stacking the finished pages until he'd made a paper tower stretching from the table to his chin.

"What are you doing in there, boy?" Papa and the other boys would ask.

To which Capote would say, "I'm writing a book." Then Papa and the other boys would laugh because the notion that someone in Monroeville, Alabama, could write a whole book was, they thought, silly, if not downright preposterous.

Capote proved my grandfather wrong and wrote many books; Papa came to admire Capote.

Papa was not especially vocal about his relationship to Lee or Capote until he retired, but once he retired, it was hard to keep him quiet about it. When I went away for college, he made a name for himself at the local high school by lecturing in my cousins' classrooms. He drawled on about Monroeville and Lee and *To Kill a Mockingbird* and specified the residents on whom Lee had based her characters. "Bubba," Nina objected more than once – Papa didn't like the nickname *Bubba*, and only Nina could call him that – "you best not tell all about the Monroeville folks. You're likely to get sued."

Papa laughed, kept giving lectures, and never got sued.

Open to the first few pages of *To Kill a Mockingbird*, and you'll see a disclaimer: "This book is a work of fiction. Names, characters, places, and incidents are the product of the author's imagination or are used fictitiously. Any resemblance to actual events, locales, persons, living or dead, is coincidental." If you had asked Papa about this disclaimer, he would have told you it was hogwash.

When I graduated from college, having earned a degree in literature, I moved to Japan to teach English. Before leaving the States, I arranged to have supper with Papa so we could talk about Harper Lee.

He and I sat at his kitchen table, in Sandy Springs, Georgia, eating boiled shrimp and drinking Nina's sweet tea, a bowl of cocktail sauce, a copy of *The Monroe Journal* (dated July 25, 2002, and headlined "A.C. Lee, the perfect 'Atticus Finch'"), and three stacks of papers between us. On one piece of paper, Papa drew a map. On another, he listed Monroevillians and their corresponding characters from *To Kill a Mockingbird*. The list looked like this:

Scout Finch..........Harper Lee
Jem Finch............Edwin Lee
Dill Harris.............Truman Capote
Atticus.................A.C. Lee
Boo Radley..........Son Boulware
Aunts...................Faulk sisters
Mr. Ewell..............Mr. Ezell
Tom Robinson.......(Fiction)
Maudie................Grandmother Mosey Neighbor
Mr. Tate, Sheriff.....Sheriff Sawyer
Calpurnia.............Georgianna
Mr. Radley............Mr. Boulware
Maycomb.............Monroeville
Macon County.......Monroe County

"This," he said, indicating a sloppy square on his map, "is the courthouse, and this is the post office." He also indicated the jail, the drug store, the elementary school; Selma Street, Montgomery Street, and Mobile Street; and some homes labeled "my home," "Grandmother (Maudie)," "Faulk," "Harper Lee," "Radley, Boo," and "Dill."

And so it went. Papa specified who lived where, why, and for how long. He explained how Amasa Coleman Lee, Harper's father, served as the model for Atticus and how Edwin Lee, Harper's brother, served as the model for Jem. He also explained how the "real" Boo Radley was Son Boulware.

The narrator of *To Kill a Mockingbird* introduces Boo as "a malevolent phantom" she had never seen but whose very breath caused azaleas to freeze "in a cold snap." She describes the Radley house as adjoining the schoolyard and declares that a "baseball hit into the Radley yard was a lost ball and no questions asked." Papa testified to the truth of this legend, saying that he and his friends would play baseball in the schoolyard and occasionally hit or throw a ball into Son Boulware's yard. They would run up to the fence to see if

41

Son would come out of the house to get the ball. He never did. But the ball would be back in the schoolyard the next morning. Papa swore that this was how Lee got the idea for the knothole in which Boo deposited gifts for Scout and Jem.

One day, when Papa was working for a Mr. Gardner, who ran a grocery store, Papa was called on to deliver a basket of groceries to Mrs. Boulware. He had told Mr. Gardner that he'd deliver groceries to anybody but the Boulwares, but Mr. Gardner would have none of it and ordered Papa to make the delivery. Papa, who had a bike with a big basket for carrying things to and from school, collected the groceries and set out for the Boulware home.

He rode up to the Boulwares' yard – which, he said, was tidy to the point of exhibitionism – and chanced his way through the gate of the picket fence, tottering up the steps to the front porch: the very porch, perhaps, that Jem had conquered to impress Scout and Dill. For some reason, Papa decided to go around to the back door; the porch, you see, stretched the length of the house. The groceries were heavy and slipping from his hands. When he turned the corner, he saw Son, or Boo, who hopped out of the porch swing and ran inside just as quickly as Papa could drop the groceries and jolt the other way. Papa always maintained that Son was "white as a sheet" that day. He rode his bike back to the grocery store and announced to Mr. Gardner that he would never deliver another thing to *that* house.

Papa used to describe the particularities and peculiarities of Mr. Boulware, Son's father, a man who never worked a steady job and who raised chickens and cultivated a beautiful vegetable garden. "He swapped chickens for groceries," Papa explained. "He'd leave his house every day, about 11:00, walking right by grandmother's, and I'd watch him sometimes from behind grandmother's shades, and he'd go three places: the post office, the courthouse, and the Jitney Jungle. He'd always return by noon."

Papa claimed that Lee modeled the character Miss Maudie on his grandmother, who would scold him and his friends when she caught them spying on the Boulwares: "Y'all leave that family alone! They've never done anything to you!"

Papa alleged, as well, that Lee modeled her characters on the following people:

Edwin Lee as Jem. Known simply as "Ed." Ed went to Auburn. That he, or anyone for that matter, went to Auburn is of tremendous significance to my family: all my grandparents – save for my paternal grandmother, who never attended college – attended Auburn; both my parents attended Auburn; my uncles attended Auburn; my sister attended Auburn; and a plethora of first, second, third, fourth, and fifth cousins attended Auburn; I earned my doctorate at Auburn. Nina's family, the Glenns, have a dorm at Auburn named for them; and Glenn Street runs through the edges of Auburn's campus.

Amasa Coleman Lee as Atticus. Harper Lee's father. A lawyer who never actually attended law school. He handled mostly wills and estates. He raised his family as Methodists and served on the board of the church. Papa heard him speak on several occasions and characterized him as a dry speaker who rattled change in his pockets while he talked.

Georgianna as Calpurnia. In the book, Calpurnia looked after Scout and Jem, but Papa claimed that that was Mrs. Lee's job and that Harper Lee had chosen not to include Mrs. Lee in the book. Georgianna was a cook who lived in a small residence behind the Lees' house. A.C. Lee did not drive her home after work, the way Atticus did for Calpurnia. Papa described Georgianna as a hefty woman who wore bright red lipstick and played the accordion in the afternoons. She was, apparently, an atrocious accordion player.

Mr. Ezell as Mr. Ewell. Ezell, like Ewell, was, in Papa's words, "poor white trash." He was an alcoholic who never worked. He and his family lived outside of town and were supported by Mrs. Ezell, who ironed, washed clothes, and undertook other odds-and-ends to make a living. Ezell's family lived in a house that someone else abandoned, and the Ezell children started school each year but always dropped out within three weeks on account of the other children laughing at them. The Ezell children never had proper clothes. Papa claimed that their family lived in that once-abandoned house until about the year he left for college. Then they disappeared, and nobody in Monroeville, at least to Papa's knowledge, knew where they went.

"Harper Lee used fake names to refer to real Monroeville people," Papa insisted. "She did it, I suspect, to avoid lawsuits." He would follow up by saying that Lee couldn't fool those who had lived in Monroeville, who had spent their days with the actual people so easily identifiable in Lee's fiction. Papa didn't know what to make of the fact that Lee had omitted some of her closest friends and relatives from the book – her sisters Alice and Marie, for example. He set aside the question by saying, "I suspect she wanted to make the book seem more like fiction."

When I was eight years old, I made a discovery much like the one Scout and Jem made about Atticus's sharpshooting skills. Nina and Papa had a Siamese cat named Susie who would sneak into the attic through unknown passageways. One afternoon, she snuck away, and I went looking for her in the upstairs bedroom. I looked under the bed, behind the shower curtain, on top of the bookcase. No Susie.

Then I saw the closet door was cracked open. I pulled it all the way open and saw a long, coffin-like case on the shelf above the clothes. I pulled it down and examined it. It was about five feet long, tapering hexagonal at the tips; it had a locked, split lid. There was nothing particularly ornamental about it, so I supposed that there was no harm in opening it. Although it was locked, its lid gave way without resistance. When that happened, I gasped, horrified, and dropped the case to the floor. My heart fluttered. Inside was a shotgun. The first I'd ever seen.

I hadn't known Papa to be a hunter or a rifleman, but when I summoned forth the courage to pick up the case and reinstate it to its proper place, I saw two or three trophies, on the shelf, that were shaped like riflemen. Apparently, Papa was a good shot.

Just as I knew nothing of Papa's marksmanship, Scout and Jem knew nothing of Atticus's marksmanship – until, that is, old Tim Johnson, a neighbor's dog struck mad with rabies, materializes in the street one afternoon, "walking dazedly in the inner rim of the curve parallel to the Radley house" and "advancing at a snail's pace." The narrator of *To Kill a Mockingbird* describes Tim Johnson as "dedicated to one course and motivated by an invisible force that was inching him toward us."

Heck Tate, the sheriff of Maycomb, surrenders his gun to Atticus, insisting that Atticus take the shot at the canine ("this is a one-shot job," Tate says). Scout and Jem watch skeptically as their father fumbles with the rifle. The reluctant Atticus – moving "like an underwater swimmer" – takes aim, pausing to adjust his glasses, which, eventually, he lets fall to the street. "With movements so swift they seemed simultaneous," the narrator says, "Atticus's hand yanked a ball-tipped lever as he brought the gun to his shoulder." Then, suddenly, Atticus eliminates the dog with a single shot, leaving Jem "paralyzed" with wonder and confused as Miss Maudie refers to Atticus as "One-Shot Finch."

"Don't you go near that dog, you understand? Don't go near him, he's just as dangerous dead as alive," Atticus tells Jem, who says, "yes, sir," and then stammers, "Atticus? – "

To which Atticus says, "Yes?"

Jem, still stunned, says, "Nothin.'"

Minutes later, Jem remains in "numb confusion" and only "vaguely articulate." Seeing this, Miss Maudie enlightens him by saying that Atticus was the best shot in Maycomb. When Jem protests that no one had told him this before, Miss Maudie muses aloud in words that, I believe, could have described my Papa:

> If your father's anything, he's civilized in his heart. Marksmanship's a gift of God, a talent – oh, you have to practice to make it perfect, but shootin's different

from playing the piano or the like. I think maybe he put his gun down when he realized that God had given him an unfair advantage over most living things. I guess he decided he wouldn't shoot till he had to, and he had to today.

I never did see Papa shoot a gun, but Nina said that one time he had shot a squirrel off the bird feeder with a BB gun because he thought birds were disadvantaged when it came to competition with the squirrels. When he went to collect the squirrel's body, the little thing came to, shook its head wildly as if snapping from a trance, and bounded away into the woods. Papa shelved the BB gun that day and never used it again.

As all grandfathers must, Papa passed on stories about his childhood, often while sitting in his reading chair with his grandkids gathered on the floor around him. "When I was a boy," he would say, "there was no swimming pool. And there was only one movie theater, and it had only one screen. They had to change the picture every day to keep business. On Saturdays, there was a double-feature: two westerns. Admission cost five cents for children, and for another five cents, you could have some popcorn." This was the world of Lee and Capote, too: the charming yet dangerous world that Lee illuminated for masses of readers.

With Lee's final tumultuous years came the passing of a part of me that I shared with my grandfather through stories. It has been said that pleasant words are like a honeycomb, sweetness to the soul and health to the bones. I know my grandfather to have been a good and honest man, and come what may, I'll tell his stories about Harper Lee and Truman Capote and Monroeville to my children and, perhaps one day, my grandchildren, that they, too, might tell their offspring. Good folks like Harper Lee and my grandfather can't be kept alive forever – Papa died a couple of years before *Go Set a Watchman* reached print – but this isn't true for the stories they leave behind. Those live. They must, for the sake of soul and bone, and for the wisdom of our posterity.

Power Made Perfect in Weakness

If we expect others to rely on our fairness and justice we must show that we rely on their fairness and justice.
— Calvin Coolidge

My wife and I recently vacationed in Florida. One morning, over a cup of coffee and a doughnut, sitting on the balcony and reading a newspaper amid seagulls and the grating roll of morning waves, I noted that one Michael Stone – a blind man, XTERRA champion, and 10-time Ironman triathlete who had recently published a book, *Eye Envy* – was to speak at the University of North Florida. I haven't read Stone's book, but it's apparently a resource for those suffering from vision loss or degenerative diseases.

Stone began to lose his sight in 2004. His blindness resulted from a rare disease called cone-rod dystrophy. Despite his handicap, he has accomplished amazing things, but not without the help of others. While racing he relies on guides, who, the newspaper explained, shout directions and warnings to him.

I'll never understand why God makes some people handicapped and others not, why some must, as a matter of course, rely on others, while some must be relied on. Like everyone, I have my theories. But they're just theories. Among them is the proposition that someday and for a time, everyone relies on someone or something and is also relied on by someone or something.

In graduate school, I took a class on Shakespeare. One of my peers was deaf. I always wanted to ask her what *that* was like, but knew that I couldn't, or shouldn't. And she, the deaf student, wouldn't *know* what it was like. Not really. Because she didn't know what it *wasn't* like. She'd never heard sounds before, at least not the way I had. She had interpreters, and I always wondered how Shakespeare's Early Modern English translated into hand signs and symbols. Every now and then another student would read a passage or recite some lines, and the deaf student, not knowing which lines were being read or recited, had to rely on her interpreter to gather meaning. I wondered how, with a split-second to think, an interpreter could sign such speech as "Cry to it, nuncle, as the cockney did to the eels when she put 'em i'th' paste alive. She knapped 'em o'th' coxcombs with a stick, and cried 'Down, wantons, down!'"

We all, deaf or not, have our limitations. But by helping one another, we limit limitations, both our own and others'. There's justice in that, to the extent justice is, as I believe, bound up with reciprocity.

Sign language is a medium of correspondence that's physical and, it seems to me, fun. It's writing in the air. I knew nothing about it as I sat in that class, but I learned to love it. Here was a system, a spatial grammar and syntax, which I saw once a week for three hours or more, over the course an entire semester, but which I couldn't comprehend by watching. It had its downsides in a graduate course. For instance, it drew attention to itself and distracted others from the text at issue. But it was beautiful.

My professor, a sweet man, tolerant to his own detriment, gave the deaf student carte blanche to do whatever she wanted. He never asked her questions and never forced her to contribute to the group conversations. And what good did this do her, or him? Part of the pleasure of graduate studies is learning to speculate openly and ferret out answers on your own. There's something unjust about taking that pleasure away from someone – about not doing your job when someone relies on you.

What, exactly, is justice to the person who has lost her hearing through no fault of her own? What ought to be the role of the one relying and the one relied on, if learning is, as it ought to be, just?

I don't know.

I can imagine being deaf, but I can't imagine being blind. One of the best essays I ever read on the subject is Borges's "Blindness." In it, Borges describes his experience as a blind man, answering questions that the curious, for whatever reason, never ask. "People," he says, "generally imagine the blind as enclosed in a black world." But people are wrong.

In fact, Borges explains, the "world of the blind is not the night that people imagine." It's actually kaleidoscopic: full of brilliant, undefined colors that may be difficult to distinguish, but that flicker and flash like poems come to life. If that's true, I understand Homer, Milton, Blacklock, and Helen Keller a little more.

The great writers and poets of the past have given us a stock of wisdom and insights that we can rely on to cultivate virtue and come to grips with life's complexities. These men and women recorded and enabled beauty and wisdom. Beauty and wisdom are just. It's also just, is it not, for God to give us some form of language with which to express ourselves and understand others – with which to cooperate.

People say that justice is blind. That may or may not be true. But the judge, as the townsfolk in Opelika, Alabama, referred to my Great-Grandfather, *was* blind – although he wasn't a judge. People just called him that for reasons unknown to me.

The judge was an erudite man who enjoyed an afternoon whisky. He would recite poetry to my grandmother, Nina, when she was a girl. Partial to the British Romantics – Wordsworth, Coleridge, and Keats – he could also quote Shakespeare, Irving, Poe, and Emerson.

I still have the judge's law books. Some of them date back to Reconstruction. Once, while thumbing through an old *Southern Reporter*, I found a folded, jaundiced sheet of paper – a place marker – wedged between some crinkling pages. On it was a poem by Abraham Lincoln. Nina says the judge kept a portrait of Lincoln in his office. This, I think, is revealing. None other than a brave man would openly admire Lincoln in Opelika during the years leading to and following the Great Depression.

If I should meet the judge one day, after death, I'll ask him whether he liked the milieu in which he lived. I'm sure he liked it as far as things went. He could know nothing else.

On second thought, if I should meet him, I'll ask him to recite poetry. Something from Wordsworth. That would be better. Certainly more beautiful.

Mr. Stone is an inspiration to those who must overcome adversity, which is to say that he is, or ought to be, an inspiration to us all. We're all handicapped to varying degrees and in ways we cannot control. Whether that's unjust is hard to say. What *is* just, though, is being there for those who rely on us.

My classmate could not have discussed Shakespeare without her tireless, interpretive intermediary, who made up for my professor's failure to teach. Borges could not have written without self-reliance, but more importantly without the influence of the great poets and, for that matter, the people who taught him the great poets. My Great-Grandfather, the Lincoln Lover, could not have memorized poetry, let alone practiced law, without someone, at some point, guiding him – and possibly without the influence of those same great poets on whom Borges relied.

The world is shot through with language and personal relations, without and in spite of which we couldn't overcome our handicaps. The justice is in the poetry; the poetry is in the making.

On that morning in Destin, as I set aside the newspaper and the sun began to rise over the powdery white sand, which was now populated by families and dashed by the rise and fall of waves, I turned to my wife and told her about Mr. Stone and his triathlons and upcoming lecture. She simply shrugged her shoulders and said, "I'm not surprised that he writes." I asked her why, and she answered, "Because writing helps us understand."

And the words and the water rolled onto shore, like a never-failing stream.

On Ugliness

I am, at this writing, looking over a spider's corpse, the little thing having spooked me into murder. It hurried across my papers at an alarming speed for so small a creature and then halted suddenly when I flinched and pushed my chair back from the desk. At this the miniature monster reared himself aloft, his front legs and chelicerae raised and ready for attack, his size strangely exaggerated. "This is *ugly*," I gasped to myself.

I've heard that spiders have thousands of eyes so it's no wonder that the thing supposed me to be threatening. I *was* threatening, whether I was one or a thousand. I reached for my newspaper and, foregoing reflection, swatted the brittle beast over and over until its yellow guts, an oozy snot-like substance, spattered all over an otherwise unblemished copy of *Cold Mountain*. I sighed, relieved and rubbing my sticky hands together, and thought, "*That was ugly*." I moved about the house looking for someone to tell about my feat.

Sometimes I short-circuit reflection, especially when, as then, an unusual thing startles me or otherwise makes me want to *tell* somebody something. I like to share my quotidian experiences with everyone, even if they won't care, and shouldn't.

I mean to say I'm a talker. It's a terrible habit, this talking. And an ugly one too. Although Freud might disagree, today's psychologists suggest that babble is a sign of a warped sense of prerogative. Folks back home simply refer to this as "diarrhea of the mouth." It's ugly.

And what an ugly feeling I get when at dinner parties people glance around the room while I'm talking to them. They're hoping, I know, that somebody will pass by and relieve them of their duties.

51

"Oh, say, have you met Jonathan?" they'll interject, grabbing poor Jonathan by the arm and stationing him in front of me. "Jonathan also went to law school. Y'all have something in common."

I might have been relating the story of my religious conversion or of my struggle with cancer but my now-retreating listener wouldn't even know. Why? Because I've chattered him out of caring. Now I'm standing there staring at an uncomfortable Jonathan whose eyes scan the room for the nearest and next substitute. He seems ugly to me, and I to him.

I used to enjoy social intercourse. Without much effort I could swap thoughts and information with people. At some point, though, I grew boring. My interests – literature, history, philosophy – didn't interest anyone else. I'm told that a good conversationalist seeks out mutual associations with others, balancing what he has to say with what others have to say. Having few things in common with others and even fewer reasons to bond, I tend to criticize or gossip or bloviate. I've read Proverbs over and over, trying to train myself into servile silence and prudent pondering. But no matter how hard I try to restrain it, my tongue wags, and out come words I wish would stay within me.

I'm loud and ugly, although not when I'm apart from humanity, alone with myself. I'm quiet then, and peaceful. Is it really so difficult to sit, silent, and to contemplate with lively joy the joys we cannot share? I love silence, and flourish in it. But the minute another human materializes I'm like a hee-hawing donkey. I grow ugly – ugly looking and ugly acting. I speak and speak and cannot stop.

I'm different when I walk and wander and wonder in nature, with no one else around. I take to the woods and trails with no companion. Rather than speak I listen: to the loud, long rattles of the woodpecker – *chrr, chrr, chrr* – and the nasal calls of the chickadee – *so-fee, so-fay, dee-day-dee*. I listen to the rush of the water in the river and think of the salmon and trout and their endless struggle against southward currents. And also of the fly-fishermen, all very old now, who frequent these secluded spaces as if they were still young boys.

Some fifteen minutes from my house the trails begin. Choked with dirt and dust, they wind northwest and terminate at a quiet cathedral of longleaf pines at the base of a small mountain, the name of which I've never bothered to learn. At this spot a prudent stroller would turn around, what with the dense foliage and snakes and spiders and wildlife. But I always chance the elements for thirty-minutes or so, straying off course to where no one, save, perhaps, a ranger, could find me. I seem to remember coming here as a child, though I couldn't say why or with whom. I seem to remember a cemetery, too, with quaint wooden gravestones, but if such things existed they've rotted away, or I've imagined them, perhaps in a dream. Not infrequently the trees in these parts begin to shudder as if annoyed or worried at my presence. On their branches some birds, watching me stumble through briars and brush, huddle in committee and chirp quietly among themselves. *"Go, go, go,"* the wind seems to whisper or whistle. And sometimes I answer, "No."

Nature is that liminal space between heaven and here. Maybe it's reflection, maybe it's liberation, but something about a walk through these trails makes me feel beautiful, or at least not ugly.

What is reflection if not a welcome inconvenience? It forces you to stop when everything about our society tells you to go. A few years ago I was driving to a job interview when an unexpected breeze swept through the car windows with a familiar fragrance: not perfume but something better. The whiff of freshly cut grass. It's strange how smells allow you to traverse space and time. Me, I travel back to my university campus and more specifically to the quad, a green and gray geometry of benches and sidewalks bristling with students who frittered away their afternoons with talk of fraternities and professors and recent sexual exploits. Or perhaps this exercise in transposition leads to my front lawn in Marietta, Georgia, where I'm young again and holding a baseball bat and taking pitches from my father, a man who never aged a day in his life and whose love for the outdoors somehow went away when the rich folks – Yankees mostly – migrated to town. These prosperous Yankees bought up the local farmland and little quaint stores, urged retail and restaurant chains upon us, and informed us, quite happily, that we were now better off.

And they were right: we *were* better off. Things were cheaper. Faster. More convenient. But there was an ancient suspicion, still with us at that time and place, that the love of money was the root of all evil, as the Good Book says, and that humans were depraved by nature and not to be trusted with riches or power or even fast-food. Our capital was mostly emotional and intellectual because we didn't have cash or luxury. Cash and luxury came later – when I was a teenager – and then went away.

Teenagers are ugly. They'll never be more beautiful than they are at present, and therefore they are ugly. Their bodies, once beyond that pubescent stage, are firmer and faster than they ever have been or will be. You'll hear people say it all the time: "He's becoming a man." And this is supposed to be a good thing? Do they mean that he, whoever he is, is growing a pot-belly and gray hair and having back aches? Of course not. So why do they say "he's becoming a man" when really they mean "he's a healthy young boy and I hope he stays that way for a long time." Very rarely do they mean "he's becoming one of us," unless, of course, the boy is already so ugly that his only chance, for want of a better word, is in adulthood. No, what they mean is that they're sad and envious: they can't be young again, can't enjoy the body in its fullest, freshest capacity.

When I say teenagers are ugly, I don't mean this boy who is becoming one of us, who already is, more or less, one of us. I mean ugly in a broader sense. I mean mood-swingin', attitude-gettin', middle-finger-flippin' ugliness. Here I must mention the teenager I saw last month. He was crossing a swell of grassy ground en route, I suppose, to the local high school, when he looked at me and began laughing. I hadn't provoked this outburst, so I didn't – and don't – know what he was laughing at. His jeans hung so low on his waist – or, rather, his legs – that I myself had a laugh at the sideways smile of his rear-end.

This teenager may have been laughing at my Roman nose, which is less pronounced now that my body has filled out and I'm no longer a scrawny, skinny youth. I used to joke about my nose until one spring, while vacationing in Mexico and wading in the pool by the wet bar, a squawking bird swooped down from a palm tree, clasping my nose in his claws, apparently mistaking his target for a loaf of bread. After this I decided my nose wasn't funny so much as grotesque. It's possible that the bird wanted to perch there, on the tip of my protuberance, to survey other tables for abandoned cheeseburgers and nachos. His purpose notwithstanding, I felt ugly when my nose began to bleed. "Don't get blood in the pool" was all that the man sitting next to me said before walking away. He, too, was embarrassed – and for himself, not me. We were both ugly.

Even after that experience I didn't realize how ugly I could be. It took a restroom mishap for me to truly understand. I had what in polite parlance is called an "emergency" at the Atlanta airport. Pushing through crowds and skipping over lines I made it just in time. I settled into a handicap stall because the "regular" stalls were taken. Then, suddenly, the door, unlocked, somehow floated open – slowly – and I sat there staring at a room full of strangers who stared back at me. When you're sitting in a handicap stall, which is much bigger than other stalls, you can't reach the door handle, no matter how long your arm is. So, panicked, and with people looking on, I stood up, waddled to the door, and closed it with a thud. In my hurry I neglected to pull up my jeans and boxers, which were still loosed around my ankles. Everyone saw, well, too much. And all of this after one guy – perhaps sympathizing with me or perhaps just disgusted – offered to shut the door *for* me. When I got to the loading ramp to board the plane, I slipped and fell on the wet floor. It had rained the night before and apparently nobody bothered to dry the area. I heard someone behind me whisper, "That's the guy from the bathroom." And I knew then that I was *very* ugly.

After the encounter with this vile and nasty spider, now a corpse rotting on my desk, something doesn't seem right. I feel guilty. As if I've done something wrong. I had never, not even for a moment, intended to take a life, but merely to rid myself of an ugly visitor. This spider, pitiful sight, as the minutes since his murder pass, becomes to me more like a monument than a mush-pile. For in his final moments he managed to arrange himself into a claw-like position, palm up to the sky. He looks like the statue of a hand. You should see him. He's beautiful. And because of my ugliness. Maybe we should all go out like this spider: quickly and without knowing it. No more ugliness or constant chatter. Just sudden peace and silence. How very, very beautiful. Imagine: somewhere, underground, we'll be like the statue of a hand, palm up to the sky – then after a few years, nothing at all.

Is Hacking the Future of Scholarship?

Most attorneys are familiar with e-discovery, a method for obtaining computer and electronic information during litigation. E-discovery has been around a long time. It has grown more complex and controversial, however, with the rise of new technologies and the growing awareness that just about anything you do online or with your devices can be made available to the public. Emails, search histories, voicemails, instant messages, text messages, call history, music playlists, private Facebook conversations and not just wall posts – if relevant to a lawsuit, these and other latent evidence, for better or worse, can be exposed, even if you think they've been hidden or discarded.

Anyone who has conducted or been involved with e-discovery realizes how much personal, privileged, and confidential information is stored on our devices. When you "delete" files and documents from your computer, they don't go away. They remain embedded in the hard drive; they may become difficult to find, but they're there. Odds are, someone can access them. Even encrypted files can be traced back to the very encryption keys that created them.

E-discovery has been used to uncover registries and cache data showing that murderers had been planning their crimes, spouses had been cheating, perverts had been downloading illegal images, and employees had been stealing or compromising sensitive company data or destroying intellectual property. Computer forensics were even used to reveal medical documents from Dr. Conrad Murray's computer during the so-called "Michael Jackson death trial."

Computer forensics can teach you a lot about a person: the websites he visits, the people he chats with, the rough drafts he abandons, the videos he watches, the advertisements he clicks, the magazines he reads, the news networks he prefers, the places he shops, the profiles he views, the songs he listens to, and so on. It's fair to say that given a laptop hard drive, a forensic expert could nearly piece together an individual's personality and perhaps come to know more about that person – secret fetishes, guilty pleasures, and criminal activities – than his friends and family do.

In light of this potential access to people's most private activities, one wonders how long it will be until academics turn to computer forensics for research purposes. This is already being done in scientific and technology fields, which is not surprising because the subject matter is the machine and not the human, but imagine what it would mean for the humanities? If Jefferson had used a computer, perhaps we would know the details of his relationship with Sally Hemings. If we could get ahold of Shakespeare's iPad, we could learn whether he wrote all those plays by himself. By analyzing da Vinci's browsing history, we might know which images he studied and which people he interacted with before and during his work on the Mona Lisa – and thus might discover her identity.

There are, of course, government safeguards in place to prevent the abuse of, and unauthorized access to, computer and electronic data: the Wiretap Act, the Pen Registers and Trap and Trace Devices Statute, and the Stored Wired and Electronic Communication Act come to mind. Not just anyone can access everything on another person's computer, at least not without some form of authorization. But what if researchers could obtain authorization to mine computer and electronic data for the personal and sensitive information of historical figures? What if computer forensics could be used in controlled settings and with the consent of the individual whose electronic data are being analyzed?

Consent, to me, is crucial: It's not controversial to turn up information on a person if he voluntarily authorized you to go snooping, never mind that you might turn up something he didn't expect you to find. But under what circumstances could computer forensics be employed on a non-consensual basis? And what sort of integrity does computer or electronic information require and deserve? Is extracting data from a person's laptop akin to drilling through a precious fresco to search for lost paintings, excavating tombs for evidence that might challenge the foundations of organized religion and modern civilization, or exhuming the bodies of dead presidents? Surely not. But *why not*?

We've been combing through the letters of our dead predecessors for some time. Even these, however, were meant for transmission and had, to that end, intended audiences. E-discovery, by contrast, provides access to things never meant to be received, let alone preserved or recorded. It's the tool that comes closest to revealing what an individual actually thinks, not just what he says he thinks, or for that matter *how* and *why* he says he thinks it. Imagine retracing the Internet browsing history of President Obama, Billy Graham, Kenneth Branagh, Martha Nussbaum, Salmon Rushdie, Nancy Pelosi, Richard Dawkins, Toni Morrison, Ai Weiwei, or Harold Bloom. Imagine reading the private emails of Bruno Latour, Ron Paul, Pope Francis, Noam Chomsky, Lady Gaga, Roger Scruton, Paul Krugman, Justice Scalia, or Queen Elizabeth II. What would you find out about your favorite novelists, poets, musicians, politicians, theologians, academics, actors, pastors, judges, and playwrights if you could expose what they did when no one else was around, when no audience was anticipated, or when they believed the details of their activity were limited to their person?

This is another reason why computer and electronic data mining is not like sifting through the notes and letters of a deceased person: having written the notes and letters, a person is aware of their content and can, before death, destroy or revise what might appear unseemly or counter to the legacy he wants to promote. Computer and electronic data, however, contain information that the person probably doesn't know exists.

More information is good; it helps us to understand our universe and the people in it. The tracking and amassing of computer and electronic data are inevitable; the extent and details of their operation, however, cannot yet be known. We should embrace –

although we don't have to celebrate – the technologies that enable us to produce this wealth of knowledge previously unattainable to scholars, even if they mean, in the end, that our heroes, idols, and mentors are demystified, their flaws and prejudices and conceits brought to light.

The question is, when will we have crossed the line? How much snooping goes too far and breaches standards of decency and respect? It's one thing for a person to leave behind a will that says, in essence, "Here's my computer. Do what you want with it. Find anything you can and tell your narrative however you wish." It's quite another thing for a person never to consent to such a search and then to pass away and have his computer scanned for revealing or incriminating data.

It's hard to say what crosses the line because it's hard to know where the line should be drawn. As Justice Potter Stewart said of hard-core pornography, "I shall not today attempt further to define the kinds of material I understand to be embraced within that shorthand description; and perhaps I could never succeed in intelligibly doing so. But I know it when I see it." Once scholars begin – and the day is coming – hacking devices to find out more about influential people, the courts and the academic community will be faced with privacy decisions to make. We'll have to ask if computer and electronic data are substantially similar to private correspondence, such as letters, to balance the need for information with the desire for privacy, to define what information is "private" or "public," and to honor the requests of those savvy enough to anticipate the consequences of this coming age of research.

Amid this ambiguity, one thing will be certain: Soon we can all join with Princess Margaret in proclaiming, "I have as much privacy as a goldfish in a bowl." That's both good and bad news.

Teaching Behind Bars

Wardens say murderers make the best students. That's because, most of the time, murderers kill out of heat-of-passion. Their crimes aren't premeditated. Their minds aren't flawed or evil. But the habitual offenders – they're the ones to worry about. They can manipulate you. They're professionals, even behind bars. I'm not saying their minds are flawed or evil – merely capable of sustained and concerted deception.

I'm a prison teacher. I teach literature. In prison, literature is currency. A book is a valuable unit of exchange. It's bought and sold, used as collateral, traded for sex. In the prison where I teach, many if not most prisoners are indigent. They shine shoes, make beds, beat up (or beat down) prisoners for nominal fees.

The books and supplies I give my students are, like drugs or weapons, contraband. Some supplies – pens, for instance – become weapons. I contribute to the system of abuse by providing goods that prisoners fight over. I do so because every class, without fail, I sense that I'm helping someone, because the pens and books usually generate thoughtful and creative essays or poems that the prisoners share with me. I do so, in other words, because the students seem to learn and reflect when I visit them. Not all of them, but enough.

At least one student, each class, appears to have a text-induced epiphany. I can tell because of what he says and how he says it, or because he thanks me so intensely, as if I might not come back next week. If I can make epiphanies happen, I've succeeded.

The first day I taught in prison, I was, as you might expect, anxious. I didn't think I would be. I wasn't anxious when I observed a prison class as part of my mandatory training – maybe because I wasn't alone then.

But I wouldn't be alone on the first day of class, either. Kyes Stevens, director of the Alabama Prison Arts and Education Project, was with me. She was to sit in on the first class, provide feedback, and then release me from her gracious supervision.

Kyes drove me to the prison that day. When I stepped onto the gravel parking lot, I didn't want to look at the naked buildings. It wasn't that I felt paralyzed under the panoptic gaze of the guard towers or victimized by the penetrating stares from the other side of the chain-linked, barbed-wire fences. I looked down because my pockets felt empty. They were supposed to be carrying my driver's license.

I patted my front pockets, and then, realizing where I left my wallet – in the glove compartment of my jeep – I pretended to check my back pockets to delay the moment when Kyes would realize my mistake.

It didn't take her long. "You forgot your wallet," she said. "Hang here. I'll talk to the chaplain. But you won't be able to get in. We'll have to drive back." I watched her shuffle into the prison office. Feeling guilty, I looked down again – and noticed a dead frog on the ground. It hadn't been dead long because its sides were rounded and fleshy and its skin still moist.

Its eyes seemed to register my presence even though neither they nor I moved. I half expected a warble to issue from its tubby belly and thick throat, but it lay still, a heart-shaped object on an unattended blanket of rock.

Suddenly Kyes returned. Relieved that my first class wouldn't be today, I was ready to apologize and get back into the car.

But she was smiling. My relief turned to worry. "We're good," she said. "Chaplain says you can come in. Just bring your ID next week."

"Good news," I lied. We went in.

I got patted down, and the guard (officer; we're supposed to call the guards "officers") made a passing remark about a cavity search, perhaps to ease the tension. Another officer shepherded us into the chapel where we were to wait until the prisoners emerged from lock-down. For some reason, three or four prisoners were with us. One of them, a heavy-set kid who couldn't have been more than 18 – but who must have been at least 18 to be in there – asked me a series of questions, first about Republicans, then about the Middle East. He said he'd been in prison for two days. He said, "This place is scary as hell," and that he'd been hiding in the chapel as long as he could. Being new myself, I felt for him.

Lock-down is a form of punishment. It happens when prisoners are caught fighting, stealing, mouthing off, smoking dope. I'm not sure why the prisoners were on lock-down that day, but I soon learned that lock-down was more normal than exceptional – at least on Thursdays around one o'clock, when I was supposed to teach.

Eventually an officer materialized and ushered Kyes and me into a classroom full of prisoners (students; we're supposed to call them "students"). The course title, "Comedy and Literature," had drawn a large crowd, but the expectant looks on several faces quickly gave way to disappointment because, I suspect, I was not what the students had hoped for: a young female graduate student. Worse, I wasn't funny, and the class was about comedy.

I tried to explain what I meant by comedy as a genre, and a few students gave their neighbors looks that seemed to mean, "This is not what I signed up for." The heavy-set kid from the chapel seemed to want to show off. He raised his hand and asked if I'd read this or that book, then declared that he'd read everything on the syllabus. I knew something wasn't right when a few students exchanged knowing glances. But I let the moment pass without comment.

Because of the lock-down, the first class was abbreviated. I felt as though I finished as soon as I began. Several students lined up to introduce themselves. One asked if I could bring him contact information for a screenwriting company because, he said, he was a professional screenwriter. Another told me about his published poetry and asked whether I wanted to see it.

I reservedly said yes. (I never saw his poetry.) Another felt the need to tell me that he was innocent and didn't belong "with these guys." Three or four others simply said, "Thank you." Thirty-three students came that day. Eleven remained on the last day of class. I never saw the heavy-set kid again. Kyes said she knew I wouldn't, that after his performance he would "get set straight." That's code for getting the shit kicked out of you.

My syllabus discussed comedy as literature, and also the role of comedy in literature. Comedy can mean many things; humor is only one aspect of the genre. My goal was for the students to learn about various expressions of comedy and how authors use comedy to comment on ethics or morality.

A course on comedy was not just for escape and relief, the syllabus explained, but for critical self-exploration. I hoped the students would develop a greater awareness of the relation of comedy to the human condition – one of those hopes that's contrary to intuition and that humanities professors recite to justify their work.

The human condition, I'm afraid, has become a tired defense for any enterprise that doesn't generate, or rarely generates, financial profit. Anyway, what was the human condition in here?

This was a place where human existence was supervised and controlled, guarded and mediated. It was cut off from the "outside" world and relegated to a strange, constant "inside."

What it meant to be inside, and how the inside was different from the outside, was something I never quite figured out, no matter how many notes I took or how many hours of reflection I went through during my drive home. I live in Atlanta. The prison is west of Montgomery, so my drives home were long.

If anything, I learned that the human condition isn't the same from time to time or place to place, and that what it means to be human, in a space where humanity isn't completely acknowledged, feels different from anything I knew. I was merely a temporary visitor with freedom of entry and exit. I wanted to be inside where "they" lived, to see the place that "they" couldn't leave, to satisfy my own curiosities – even as I wanted to help them learn to better themselves.

I sometimes wonder whether the prisoners' bored lives were a perverse source of pleasure for me. I appreciated my life, and the decisions I had made, more and more each class. For every good motive there is an ulterior one, and sometimes motives are sublimated. And even if I did good things by teaching in prison, even if my motives were, for lack of a better word, pure, I feel, in some ways, guilty for the smugness that I assumed when I left – and that I tried, unsuccessfully, to fight off. During the drives to and from prison, I asked myself why teaching there made me feel good about myself. Was it because I was doing something for others, or for me? Did it matter? What was the difference?

One day I distributed copies of J. M. Coetzee's *Disgrace*, most of which I never saw again. I expected that. The book opens with sex, and sex recurs throughout. Sex, in a place where it's forbidden, where it's either coerced or a last resort, is a luxury worth hiding and fighting for.

It's in high demand and short supply. It's the thing prisoners miss most. I'm not sure what happened to those books, but I'm sure they were put to use, sold, fought over. I don't give extra supplies. I provide students with what they need and nothing more, because if they get more, they'll harm others and themselves.

And if that happens, the guards – officers – will begin to see the teachers as a problem. And if the teachers become problems, they disappear. Quickly.

I didn't want to disappear. Murderers make the best students. They didn't want me to disappear, either.

Most university students take my course because literature is a requirement, a hurdle over which they must jump if they want to graduate. To get them to read, I threaten them with pop quizzes or bribe them with bonus points. I tell them I'm grading them. Most of them hate literature. They think they know what's important to learn, and it isn't poetry or philosophy or Great Books. They view literature as something like punishment.

But the prisoners, the people whose lives have become punishment, are willing to circulate petitions to have more literature classes and to stake their reputations on literature, which is, in a space of perpetual confinement, the opposite of punishment – the closest thing to sex that isn't sex itself.

My university students complete their writing assignments because they are mandatory and graded. I don't give my prison students writing assignments, but every week the prisoners give me a stack of essays they've written. They like writing, and reading. And they like Shakespeare. And they like me.

Why, I ask again, does teaching in prison make me feel good about myself? Is it because I'm doing something for others, or for me? Does it matter? What's the difference?

I'm a creature of habit. I establish routines and stick to them. Each week on my way to the prison I stopped at Dairy Queen, an indulgence that struck me as inappropriate after one of my students told me that a visiting relative had brought him a Burger King hamburger – the first hamburger he'd eaten since being admitted 15 years ago.

Every week that first semester I arrived at the same time, parked in the same spot. Every week I looked down at the frog corpse, which nobody had touched. It decayed a little more each time I studied it. It was like a piece of garbage that no one would throw away. I had a hard time imagining it ever lived.

One week I wasn't allowed inside. I waited for two hours in the front office before giving up and going home. The next week, I learned there had been a stabbing. Apparently, two prisoners got in a fight, one stabbed the other, the wounded one ducked into a dorm so his pals could stitch him up, and the guards walked in as the stitching was taking place. The prison went on lock-down.

When I saw my students the next week, they apologized. But it wasn't their fault. To my knowledge, no one in the class was involved in the fight. Nevertheless, I let them apologize because I was afraid of what they would say or do if I yielded authority. I couldn't let them know they were in control.

Moments like this made me wonder what these men were like when I wasn't around. They couldn't be this polite and enthusiastic around other prisoners, could they? Were they special prisoners, the ones whose love for literature had cultivated moral sensitivity?

Perhaps it was a performance. The only people who didn't seem to perform in prison were the guards (officers). We didn't trust each other. To them, I was probably a bleeding heart liberal who thought he could change a bunch of hardened criminals. To me, they were a mob of jocks who made a display of their callousness and cruelty, saying things like, "Our job would be easier if we could kill them all off," or "Which dude are you gonna set straight today?" Never mind that the officers were victims of desensitization and may not have played sports at all.

Perspective is a funny thing. I'm sure the officers were fine men individually, but when they were together they traded crude jokes, mocked the prisoners, and laughed uproariously at either my or the prisoners' expense. One day an officer taunted me with questions about my "comfy" life in the "ivory tower," and about the pointlessness of literature.

I sat there, silent, taking it all in, because I didn't know what else to do, and because, to a certain extent, I was used to it, what with my university students being so disdainful of literature. I even agreed with the officer on some points. I have reservations about the utility of literature, and I have a save-the-world-on-your-own-time mentality in the classroom.

The only bad thing that happened to me in prison was that a guard stole my leather keychain, which my sister had given me as a Christmas present. I wasn't upset because I lost the keychain. It was the principle of the matter.

Taxpayers were supporting the officers to protect people like me, but the officers were stealing from me – doing what some prisoners had done to get there in the first place. This wasn't right, but it was routine. And routine is order.

The students were clearly disappointed about missing class because of the stabbing.

They wanted to talk. They wanted new reading assignments. Two weeks after the stabbing, they came to me with a proposal. Would I, they asked, take their petition supporting more prison classes and give it to Kyes?

They explained that the only opportunity for intellectual fulfillment was during my class. No other classes were offered, and the students wanted to read more than I could provide. One wanted to learn French, another to study Western political philosophy, still another to translate something from Latin to English.

They wanted me to see if Kyes could establish something like a school in prison. Although I nodded enthusiastically, I realized they were growing delusional the more they talked about what they wanted, that they were fantasizing about a knowledge exchange that could never happen.

They wanted school to come to them. Most of my university students wanted out of school. What made my prison students different? Was it time or banality? Was it that they had nothing else to do?

Perhaps. But when I think about the sincerity and intensity with which they approached literature, I shudder to think that my university students aren't as willing or appreciative. Then again, my university students, for all their snarky and selfish attitudes, weren't criminals or murderers. And I suppose that not all prison students were in my class for the "right" reasons. Some wanted to mix up the routine, and some wanted to avoid the violence and futility of prison life. My course gave them focus and meaning. If only my university students could realize this potential in texts.

I taught *Waiting for Godot* in my prison class. Afterward a balding white man, in prison for cocaine, pulled me aside and said, "Hey, man, I know this is a comedy course, but that play was a little too real for the guys in here – because we actually know what it is to wait for Godot."

And here I thought the play was absurd. It all comes down to futility. If my class provided focus and meaning, what did it mean that I taught a text on meaninglessness? That's a vulgar reading of the play, but try finding meaning in meaninglessness when you're behind bars. It's easy to forget where you are when you teach in prison. The classroom itself is separate from the quotidian realities of prison life. It's an artificial space. The prisoners attend my class to escape, but the classroom is, architecturally and geographically, right in the middle of the prison. No place besides my class is more central – physically, functionally and metaphorically – because without my class prisoners would feel confined beyond their tolerance level.

No matter how much I want my classes to be about intellectual fulfillment, self-improvement or aesthetic appreciation, they always serve another function: to keep prisoners from thinking about their confinement. If my class is escapist, what it escapes is not physical reality but habits of thinking. Is it problematic that my class both enables and perpetuates psychological torment at the same time it provides temporary relief? If my class helps the system run, and run well, isn't it strange that the class is putatively about escape from the system?

Routine is order.

When I pulled my jeep into the parking lot for the last day of my first semester, something felt strange. At first I couldn't figure out what. Then I realized that the lot had been paved. No more gravel. The ground was smooth and black and hot.

It was May now, and May in Alabama is like July in other states. You could see steam rising from the asphalt. I looked down where the frog was supposed to be. It wasn't there. For 14 weeks it had been there, undisturbed. Now it was gone. As I waited to be admitted, I thought back on the semester and all my victories and failures. I thought about one student who'd succeeded in getting his crossword puzzle accepted for publication in the *Los Angeles Times*, and about another whose short story had been published in a prominent literary magazine. Then I thought about the student whose poetry I had agreed to read but never actually read. That student quit coming to class. I thought I must have offended or disappointed him because of my own fear and false sense of superiority. I tried, sitting there, to justify my arrogant behavior on the grounds that I was still here in prison, still doing something decent and right, still helping prisoners to learn.

But putting yourself into a situation to do good is not the same as doing good.

We watched a film during the last class. I distributed certificates of completion, and after the film I gave my obligatory departure speech. Prison teachers are shuffled from facility to facility to avoid longstanding relationships with students. I knew I wouldn't be back in this prison and that I'd never see these students again, unless they got out one day and thought to look me up.

I hadn't planned a speech. I never plan speeches. "In the outside world," I said, "people don't watch as much news or read as many books as you do. I can't get my freshmen to read anything unless I give them pop quizzes. They complain when I assign something longer than four pages. And I teach at a nationally recognized institution."

The speech was degenerating into something about me, not about them, but they didn't seem to mind. I think they understood that, all along, the class, for me, had been partially about me, even as it was about them, too.

The students listened intently as I told them how my university freshmen had bragged about not reading and had told me, more than once, that they thought poetry was pointless and that literature wasn't worth studying.

I couldn't tell if the prisoners were shocked or mad or sad. Maybe they were pained to learn that the outside world might not care about what they were doing in my classroom. Maybe they resented that others looked down on a thing – literature – that they had come to practice and love. Maybe they couldn't understand why anyone on the outside would neglect something so precious as knowledge or literature.

Or maybe they could understand, and that's what hurt the most: knowing they'd lost the freedom not to care.

To Educate in the Permanent Things

In a recent State of the Union address, President Obama proposed changes to preschool, high school, and college education, respectively. His proposals generated praise and condemnation from the predictable cheerleaders and naysayers. Some celebrated his efforts to expand early childhood education; others suggested he should have focused more on the student loan crisis; still others, not to be outdone, pointed to school funding, teacher salaries, grading, standardized testing, technology, and foreign study as the pressing issues that he neglected to address with sufficient detail.

Everyone, it seems, has an opinion about how to improve American education from the top down. But positive change rarely happens through centralized design; it arises spontaneously through the interaction of human agents operating within and among social groups. The State cannot plan and then promulgate a proper education, and legislative enactments cannot reflect the mores and traditions of local groups with differing standards and expectations. The most prudent and humble proposals for improving education are not couched in statist, Platonic terms about civic education and human perfection; instead, they approach learning modestly, on the individual level. They entail the everyday interactions between teachers and students. They are not stamped with the approval of politicians, unions, think tanks, or interest groups. They take place in the classroom, not the public square. A teacher anywhere, whatever his station, school, or background, can implement them in his course without disrupting the pace or provoking the ire of the educational establishment. The best of these, because it is so easily executed, is simply to teach what T.S. Eliot, and Russell Kirk after him, called "permanent things."

The permanent things are the inherited principles, mores, customs, and traditions that sustain humane thinking and preserve civilized existence for future generations; their canonization in literary, philosophical, religious, and historical texts happened and is happening in slow degrees. We can trace the permanent things through curricula that emphasize the ultimate values of prosperous societies. An informed, laborious study of the perennial themes and archetypal patterns in what are variously denominated as the Great Works, the Western Canon, or the Classics can help us to organize and make sense of the permanent things. There are those who would object that this approach seems too hopeful and ideal. But no one has suggested it as a panacea, of which there are none, and anyway, is there a proposal that could be simpler, more straightforward, and more workable than assigning and discussing the Great Works?

As early as 1948, Eliot remarked that "there is no doubt that in our headlong rush to educate everybody, we are lowering our standards, and more and more abandoning the study of those subjects by which the essentials of our culture – of that part of it which is transmittable by education – are transmitted; destroying our ancient edifices to make ready the ground upon which the barbarian nomads of the future will encamp in their mechanized caravans." It might be asked just who these barbarian nomads are and why we ought not to welcome their cultural practices and assumptions. The barbarian nomads could be, I think, any group lacking in historical perspective and mostly ignorant of the illuminating continuities that have guided our weightiest and most imaginative thinkers. The practices and assumptions of these nomads are not grounded in lived experience but aimed at utopian projects such as ensuring equality, creating fundamental rights, or eliminating poverty, and, to the extent that these practices and assumptions deviate from enduring norms, they cannot be said to have flourished ever.

To study the permanent things, on the other hand, is to consider the prevailing and profound ideas from certain times and schools in relation to other such ideas from various times and schools throughout successive eras. It is to map the course of perennial ideas to examine how they apply to different settings and generations. It is both sequential and diachronic in its approach. Its chief benefit is to put ideas into context, which is to say that it is to make us aware of our own presuppositions and perspectives that necessarily arise from our social, cultural, and historical situation. Each thinker lives in his own specific era and place and cannot gain knowledge in a vacuum outside of time; our era and place shape the manner in which we think and restrict our ability to imagine conditions beyond our immediate and tangible experience.

This is not to submit that our ideas are determined for us, only that we enter into experience with certain perceptions that we have no control over. They are there because of the conditions present at the time and space in which we exist. A sustained study of the permanent things will show us that our perceptions are not totally alien from those of our predecessors, although the respective perceptions are different. It also teaches us to compensate for our prejudices and to avoid thinking that our necessarily limited perspectives are unconditionally true and universally acceptable, even if they have verifiable antecedents. It reveals, as well, that schools of thought cannot simply be deemed later versions of earlier schools just because the two are in agreement about certain points. Finally, although we cannot escape those presuppositions that are embedded in our thought and culture, being alert to their probable existence can counteract their possible effect.

A rigorous study of the permanent things provides a lodestar for evaluating particular ideas against that which has been tested and tried before. Ideas that seem new always have traceable antecedents, and individuals equipped with a fundamental knowledge of the permanent things are able to situate purportedly novel ideas alongside their forerunners. These individuals recognize that change is not always progress; sometimes it is decline, deterioration, or decay. Only a sense of the continuities of history and thought can demonstrate the difference. Our political pedants in general and President Obama in particular insist on recognizing and implementing new institutions as if a radical departure from historic standards and established customs is itself the mark of good and lasting policy. Yet the permanent things show that even the most exceptional thinkers, those who represent the spirit of their age, whatever that might have been or might be, are part of a greater tradition.

It may be true that to study a particular thinker's cultural milieu and biography is requisite to placing his ideas into their proper context and highlighting the unacceptable premises of his philosophy; nevertheless, cautious interpreters ought to consider whether his thoughts necessarily lead to certain consequences, or whether the events that seem related to his thoughts arose accidentally, apart from his philosophy. Put another way, the cautious interpreter must carefully consider causation: whether theories actually generate particular circumstances, or whether those circumstances would have come to pass regardless of what the thinker spoke or wrote. Mussolini, for instance, praised William James, but it does not follow that anything James said or wrote endorses or enables fascism. He who would suggest otherwise betrays an ignorance of James's work. The permanent things can help us to distinguish the true forms and implications of an individual's thought from their appropriations by hostile forces.

By studying the permanent things, we learn that we cannot achieve a proper education through mere funding; nor does the solution to schooling gridlock and setbacks come from student aid, dress codes, student evaluations, tuition, or whatever. These issues begin to seem fleeting and trivial to one with an historical sense. They are at most temporary struggles, and although they are important, as all struggles are important, we are not to subordinate liberal learning to them. The best way to achieve the liberal learning necessary to make important and meaningful distinctions about our complex world is, as I have suggested and as it bears repeating, through a holistic, painstaking exploration of the permanent things. This means not only reading the Great Works for their content, but analyzing them in light of their place in history.

The beauty of this approach is that anyone can carry it out; the wisdom of it lies in its civilizing effects. Whether one is a homeschooling parent, a public school teacher, the leader of a local book club, or simply a curious-minded autodidact, the permanent things are available to him in texts, waiting to be sifted through and analyzed. It is true that there is disagreement as to what constitutes a Great Work and by what criteria, but it does not take more than research and commonsense empiricism to discern which pre-twentieth century texts have withstood the test of time. Teaching the permanent things does not require a large-scale, bureaucratic, administrative overhaul. It does not demand central planning or the implementation of mass, curricular programs; it can be accomplished through decentralized networks of concerned individuals. If parents would teach their children, friends their friends, colleagues their colleagues, and so on, we would in the aggregate become a more literate, astute, and informed society. And as our politicians lecture us about our duties even as they demand our money, we can take comfort in the proverb that these things too shall pass.

About the Author

Allen Mendenhall is associate dean at Thomas Goode Jones School of Law, executive director of the Blackstone & Burke Center for Law & Liberty, and editor of *Southern Literary Review*. Visit his website at AllenMendenhall.com.

CPSIA information can be obtained
at www.ICGtesting.com
Printed in the USA
BVOW09s0049270517
485054BV00001B/15/P